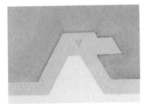

"Watch the heartbeat in your wrist --
a precise pulsing beat of life's Drum --
with loss of timing you are ill."

Jimalee Burton, Cherokee

For Bill Kauth,
a first man in his own right.
C.R.

Published by Troll Communications L.L.C.

Published by arrangement with The Rourke Corporation, Inc.

This edition published in 2001.

First paperback edition published 1998.

Printed in the United States of America.

10   9   8   7   6   5   4

Library of Congress Cataloging-in-Publication Data

Dominic, Gloria, 1950-
     First Woman and the Strawberry: a Cherokee Legend/by Gloria Dominic; illustrated by Charles Reasoner.
     p. cm.—(Native American lore and legends)
     Includes bibliographical references.
     Summary: Tells the story of an argument between First Man and First Woman and how the first strawberry was created.
     ISBN 0-86593-431-2 (lib. bdg.)   ISBN 0-8167-4513-7 (pbk.)
     1. Cherokee Indians—Folklore. [1. Cherokee Indians—Folklore. 2. Indians of North America—Folklore. 3. Strawberries—Folklore.] I. Reasoner, Charles, ill.   II. Title.   III. Series.
E99.C5F57 1996
398.2'08997—dc20   96-9040
                                                                                                CIP
                                                                                                 AC

Designed by Susan and Dave Albers

■ NATIVE AMERICAN LORE & LEGENDS ■

FIRST WOMAN

AND THE STRAWBERRY

A CHEROKEE LEGEND

ADAPTED AND RETOLD BY GLORIA DOMINIC

ILLUSTRATED BY CHARLES REASONER

Troll

One day, Grandmother sat with her granddaughter. Spring was in bloom all around them. The grass was tender and fresh. Tree buds were opening, their light green leaves unfurling to catch the sun.

"Do you know what I would like right now?" Grandmother asked. "A ripe, red, sweet strawberry."

"I would like one, too," said her granddaughter. "They are so delicious!"

"Did you know that Great Spirit made the first strawberries especially for a Cherokee woman?" Grandmother asked.

"What do you mean?" asked the girl.

"Listen closely, and I will tell you," answered the old woman.

Long ago, First Woman and First Man lived happily together. Each day they searched the forest, finding beauty all around them. They listened to the birds sing. They watched the many animals of the forest. They discovered silvery fish splashing in ponds and streams. They saw colorful birds fly across the sky.

First Woman and First Man
always helped each other. One warm
spring day, the couple walked together,
carrying beautiful baskets that First Woman had woven.
They entered the forest in search of spring's first tender roots,
which they planned to gather in their baskets.

he two had not gone far when they reached a fork in the path. "Let us go this way," suggested First Woman, pointing to the right. "I hear many squirrels calling. There are sure to be tender roots where the squirrels dig."

"No," said First Man. He pointed to the other path. "Let's go this way. I have been down this path before and have always found roots and nuts there."

"Why shouldn't we try another way?" insisted the woman.

But the man would not agree. So like many troubles that grow big from small, the two began to argue.

At last, the woman grew so impatient that she threw her hands up and said, "Bah! I am going my way whether you come along or not!" She set off quickly along the path she had chosen.

"Go ahead," called the man angrily. "It makes no difference to me!" Stubbornly, he crossed his arms and watched as First Woman's figure grew smaller and smaller in the distance.

"What do I care?" First Man asked himself. He sat down on the ground, eating one of the roots the two had already gathered. Strangely, he found he had very little appetite. At first, he thought it was because he was still angry. But soon the man realized he was lonely.

"She is gone only a short time and I miss her already," he muttered. "It was a silly fight. Perhaps if I go now, I'll be able to catch up to her."

The man set off, traveling as fast as he could. But he could not keep up with First Woman. Her anger still burned inside her, making her walk very fast.

A deer saw First Man hurrying along. "Run," the animal said. "Run as quickly as a deer." The man tried, but he could not catch up to the woman.

Then a large crow saw the man. He cawed loudly. "Listen to me," said the bird to First Man. "Call her name loudly! Call as loudly as a crow."

Nothing else seemed to be working, so First Man called after the woman. Over and over, he called her name in a loud voice. But if First Woman heard him, she did not turn around.

The man was about to give up when a fish in the stream shouted to him. "First Man, look here!" the fish said. "Jump in the water and swim after her. The water will carry you as quickly as a fish."

First Man did as the fish suggested. He swam quickly along. But still he could not reach her.

At last, exhausted, the man climbed out of the water and sat down to rest. "I will never catch up to her," he said, discouraged.

To his surprise, a voice unlike any other spoke to him. "Do not give up," the voice said. "Although you are tired, go after her. I will help you."

First Man knew this was the voice of the Great Spirit. First Man did not know how he could possibly overtake First Woman. But he did as Great Spirit told him, setting off on the road once again.

"I will go ahead of you and slow First Woman down," Great Spirit said.

He decided to attract her attention with a bit of spring's bounty. So along the trail where First Woman walked, Great Spirit made a vine grow, full of luscious purple grapes. The woman saw the grapes, but she was too angry to stop.

"That is strange," said Great Spirit. "Let me try something else." He made a wild cherry tree grow. Upon its low branches hung dark fruit, just where First Woman would be sure to see it.

First Woman saw the cherries, but she did not stop to pick them.

Next Great Spirit caused bushes filled with huckleberries to grow across the path. The woman continued on, pushing through the bushes. She saw the berry juice stain her clothes, but still she did not stop to taste the berries.

Great Spirit was truly amazed at the strength of First Woman's anger. He had one more idea. "I will create a completely new berry," he said. "Its odor will be irresistible. This new berry will grow close to the ground—and it will be delicious."

So Great Spirit created the first strawberries. They grew in short tangles upon the ground where the woman walked.

First Woman did not notice the plants as she hurried along. But before long, she stumbled upon the low vines. She tumbled to the ground, crushing several of the ripe strawberries.

"What is that sweet smell?" thought First Woman as she sat up. "I have never smelled it before."

The woman looked down and saw the beautiful color of the fruit. "Never have I seen a red so lovely," she said. "I wonder how these pretty berries taste."

Picking the biggest strawberry she could find, First Woman ate it. The delicious taste filled her mouth, and she instantly forgot her anger. "This is surely the most wonderful-tasting berry in all the forest," she said. She quickly ate several more.

All at once, the woman had an idea. After she'd eaten her fill of the tempting fruit, First Woman gathered more, filling her basket. Then she turned back along the path, walking almost as quickly as before. As she walked, the animals saw her.

A deer called out, "What are you carrying?"

"A treasure!" answered First Woman. "Try one." She tossed a berry to the deer and hurried along.

Soon a crow called to the woman. "What is in your basket?" he asked.

"A gift," said the woman. "But you may have one." She held up a strawberry for the bird, who gobbled it hungrily.

T hen First Woman heard a voice unlike any other. She knew it was the Great Spirit. "Where are you going?" he asked. "I must find First Man," she answered. "I have something special to share with him."

"Are you still angry with him?" asked Great Spirit.

"No," said First Woman. "The sweetness of these berries has reminded me of the sweetness of our love."

It was not long before First Man and First Woman met each other along the path. First Woman excitedly showed the strawberries to her husband. The two ate the fruit. It was the most delicious meal they had ever shared. The two embraced, their anger forgotten.

First Woman and First Man returned to their home in the forest. They lived together very happily for the rest of their days. Each spring, the husband and wife went out to search for the first strawberries, which they gave to each other as a gift. First Woman learned to make many wonderful things from the strawberries, including sweet-tasting jellies and jams to eat all year round. If they were ever to quarrel, these delicious foods were always there to remind them of their love for each other.

"That is how the first strawberries were created," concluded Grandmother. "It is also why many women still keep strawberries in the kitchen of their happy homes."

"Can we find some, too?" asked the little girl.

"Very well," agreed Grandmother.

So the old woman and her granddaughter set off to find the first sweet strawberries of spring.

The Cherokee

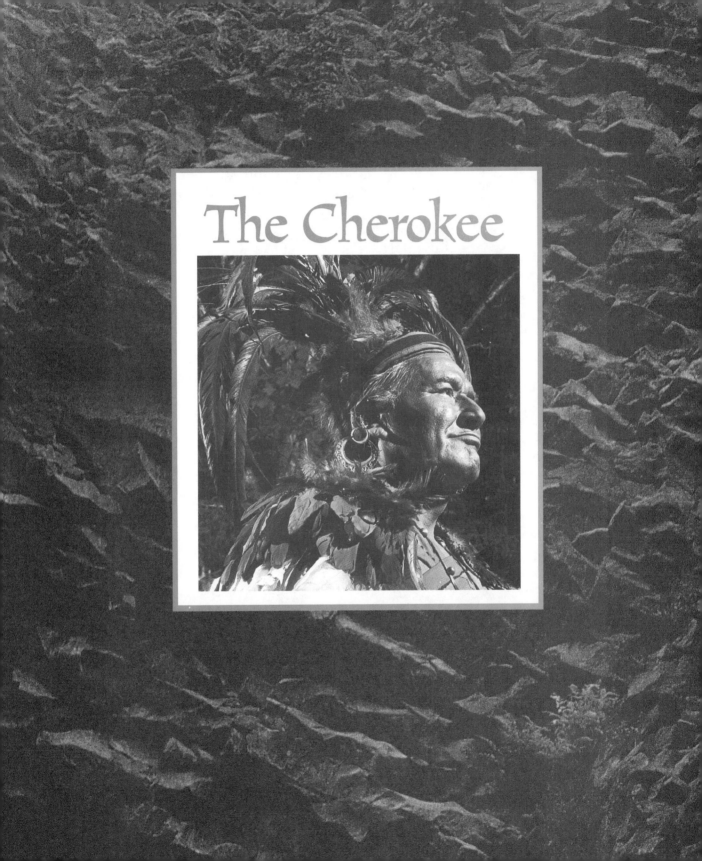

TRAIL OF TEARS

WATER ROUTE   LAND ROUTES

OHIO

ILLINOIS   INDIANA

MISSOURI

KANSAS

KENTUCKY

TENNESSEE

NORTH
CAROL

OKLAHOMA

ARKANSAS

GEORGIA

MISSISSIPPI

ALABAMA

TEXAS

FLORIDA

LOUISIANA

GULF OF MEXICO

THE CHEROKEE

The Five Civilized Tribes

Long ago, the Cherokee lived a good life in the mountainous areas of present-day Georgia, Tennessee, and North Carolina. But the arrival of the Europeans changed everything. By the late nineteenth century, the Cherokee way of life was gone forever.

After the American Revolution, the new country steadily ate away at the Cherokee homeland. The U.S. government decided to "help" the natives through a "civilization" policy. "Civilization" to the white men meant teaching the natives to be more like them. Due to their successful efforts in becoming "good neighbors," the Cherokee, along with the Chickasaw, Choctaw, Creek, and Seminole, are known as the Five Civilized Tribes.

Below. A log cabin scene from Oconaluftee Indian Village of Cherokee, North Carolina. The village is a replica of a 1750 Cherokee community.

PROTECTION

ᏣᎳᎩ ᏧᎴᎯᏌᏅᎯ

CHEROKEE PHŒNIX. 17

VOL. I. NEW ECHOTA, WEDNESDAY AUGUST 6, 1828. NO

[ED]ITED BY ELIAS BOUDINOTT.
PRINTED WEEKLY BY
ISAAC H. HARRIS,
FOR THE CHEROKEE NATION.

...tinues for a year, and takes place upon the death of parents. The children do not put on black, but are obliged to wear, during the whole year, the clothes which they had on at the death of their father, without being allowed to change them, let them be ever so tattered. They fast on the anniversary of his death, every year. Second mourning lasts a month, and takes place on the demise of children, uncles, aunts. During that period they dare neither wash themselves, shave, nor perfume themselves, nor even cut their nails. They ...

...doubt, sir, that you have yours."—"Yes, sir, I am a man catcher."—"A man catcher, (said the gentleman, are you? I am glad to hear you say so, for you are the very person I want. I am a justice of the peace in this district, and am commissioned to seize the person of Dick Baxter, who is expected to preach at a conventicle in this neighborhood early to-morrow morning; you shall go with me, and I doubt not we shall easily apprehend the rogue." Mr. B. agreed to accompany him. Accordingly, the next morning, the gentleman took Mr. Baxter in his carriage to the place where the meeting was to be held. When they arrived at the spot, they saw a considerable number of people, hovering about, for seeing the carriage of the justice, and suspecting his intentions, they were afraid to enter the house. The justice observing this, said, to Mr. Baxter, "I am afraid they have obtained information of my design; Baxter has probably been apprised of it, and will not fulfil his engagements; for you see the people will not enter into the house. I think if we extend our ride a little farther, our departure may encourage them to assemble, and on our return we may fulfil our commission." When they returned, they found their efforts useless, for the people still appeared unwilling to assemble. The magistrate, thinking he ...

...ly the whole of Europe experienced, in some degree, the earth's commotion. The cities we have alluded to above, were those where the shock was the severest. Liege being undermined in its whole extent by coal pits, its inhabitants were greatly as justly terrified. At Maestrecht, a catholic priest was in the act of performing the burial service in the public cemetery, placed, as it would seem, on the very line the earthquake most forcibly evinced itself. Alarmed at the unaccountable phenomenon, he, with the mourners, most unceremoniously left 'the dead to bury the dead,' and took to his heels, none of the party pausing to take breath until they had attained the town. At Tongres, the mass for the dead was saying in the ancient and remarkable church of that oldest of the cities of the Netherlands; and the corpse of a young woman was lying before the altar, when the coffin was observed to move upon the tressels that supported it, and a strange moaning sound was heard to fill the church: unprepared for these unusual events, fear got the better of devotion. Without the 'let us start fair' formality of the Cornish Curate, the Priest headed his flock in the attempt to escape from the church, but the doors opening inward, were at once closed by the rush of the affrighted congregation; and long and fearful was the struggle, and the cries and shrieks of the candidates for *Catholic Emancipation* most alarming, ere a *sortie* could be effected.

...OOD AT ST. PETERSBURGH.

...llowing account of the flood ...tersburgh, ... Wilson in his "Travels in ...

...served. A wooden ho... lifted from its founda... and washed into the ... and on searching this, ... contain much property ... ter subsiding, the dea... male was found kneeli... supplicating to the ima... fixed to the wall. ... city all was terrour, ... may; for the terrified ... agined a general delug... take place."

From the N. Y. Journ...

Some things can be ... others.—On Friday la... 4 P. M. agreeable to ... hair-brained fellow in ... name we do not recoll... the Passaic Falls ju... idle whim of his own... third time he has do... time he did it privatel... periment—he then ... would do it publicly f... tion of any who please... The authorities in ... justly alarmed, & put ... ing till they supposed ... ed the purpose, but ... opportunity after be... restraint, and when ... sons were present, in ... sition, he carried it in... Since that time the ... allowed him to cons... safety, and he leaps ... of a hundred feet wh... his fancy. It does no... receives or expects ... for performing this d...

Top. The August 6, 1828, edition of the Cherokee Phoenix *newspaper, which was printed in both English and Sequoyah's syllabary.*

Left. Sequoyah was considered one of the greatest Cherokee because he is the only known man to create an alphabet by himself.

Children went to school and learned English. Men turned family farms into small plantations. Women made clothing out of woven cloth instead of animal skins. A Cherokee man named Sequoyah created an alphabet based on their spoken language, and most of the population became literate within a few years.

Then gold was discovered in Georgia, and thousands of greedy settlers poured into the Cherokee homeland. In 1830, the Indian Removal Act gave President Andrew Jackson the right to move the Five Civilized Tribes west to Indian Territory (which later became part of Oklahoma) and take their land. Principal Chief John Ross fought injustices through the U.S. court system and won. But President Jackson and Congress continued to strip away Cherokee rights.

Over the next several years, Ross repeatedly tried to negotiate with the U.S. government, without success. While Ross was away in 1835, a small group of Cherokees and their leader, Major Ridge, signed away all of the Cherokees' rights to their homeland. Ross went to Washington with a treaty signed by more than fifteen thousand Cherokees protesting the treaty that Ridge had signed. But it was useless, and removal began soon after.

Right. The sequoia tree - named in honor of Sequoyah - may reach over 300 feet in height.

Trail of Tears

In 1838, government troops invaded the Cherokee Nation and moved people into stockades (enclosed camps). A few soldiers allowed people to gather belongings and find loved ones, but most did not. Many natives had nothing but the clothes they wore.

Large numbers of Cherokees became sick and died in the stockades. Three groups moved west in the sweltering summer heat, by boat and on foot, to disastrous results. Ross requested permission to organize his people's relocation. He obtained wagons, horses, and supplies, divided the people into thirteen groups, and assigned trusted leaders. Some rode, but most walked the twelve hundred miles through five states, carrying what little they had left. Along the way, the people encountered snow, rain, and freezing cold; all kinds of diseases; exhaustion and exposure; lack of supplies; unsanitary conditions; and greedy and cruel white settlers.

Ross led the last party, which arrived in March 1839. Of the fourteen thousand who started the march, one in four died—about four thousand people total. Every family lost someone, including Ross, whose beloved wife died. For this reason, the trip is known as "nuno dunatlohila," which means "the trail where they cried." It is also known as the Trail of Tears.

Below. To Native American people, North America was a turtle's back, which they lived on and called Turtle Island. They used the turtle in many of their ritual objects, like this rattle.

Top. Dressed in brighter colors than his ancestors, Thomas Muskrat teaches his grandson, Justin, Cherokee dances.

Left. Teachers and their helpers at the Cherokee Female Seminary in Tahlequah, Oklahoma, around 1890.

Life in Oklahoma

Life in Indian Territory was not easy. Fierce fighting among the different groups threatened to divide the Cherokee forever. Ross worked hard to bring everyone together to build a new life. By 1846, there was a united Cherokee Nation with a capital in Tahlequah. They coaxed crops out of the dry, flat land and opened schools and seminaries for their children. Some schools were better than the nearby ones for white children. Many Cherokee students finished their education at universities such as Princeton.

Cherokee Today

Today Cherokee people live in non-native cities and on reservations in Oklahoma and North Carolina. One of the largest groups of Native Americans in the United States, the Cherokee maintain a successful self-government. Many work recreating traditional crafts, while others work in non-native industries, such as timber, tourism, the arts, and sciences.

Above. Cherokee women potters in North Carolina.

Left. A Cherokee-designed ceramic pot.

Right. Loretta Galcatcher, an employee of Cherokee Nation Industries, inspects a circuit board for defects. The board will be used on a rocket launcher.

40

Above. Scene from Oconaluftee Indian Village of a craftsman making a dug-out canoe using an axe and fire.

Glossary

Ani-ya-wiya: The Cherokee's name for themselves, meaning "Real People"

Cede: To transfer ownership of land by treaty

Cherokee: From Choctaw "Chilak-ki," meaning "mountain or cave people"

The Eastern Band: Descendants from small groups of Cherokees who stayed in the Southeast or fled from the Trail of Tears. Their headquarters are in North Carolina.

Nuno Dunatlohila: The Cherokee name for the Trail of Tears, meaning "the trail where they cried"

Stockades: Enclosures made of wood, usually to hold prisoners

Syllabary: A type of alphabet using a symbol for each syllable sound

The Western Band: Descendants from the survivors of the Trail of Tears. Their headquarters are in Oklahoma.

Right. Detail of a scene from Oconaluftee Indian Village of a Cherokee using a deer antler to chip arrowheads.

Left. Arrowheads similar to this were used when hunting and fighting.

43

Above. The Citizenship Committee for the Cherokee Nation for the Dawes enrollment. The enrollment was from 1899 to 1906. Clem Rogers (back row, farthest left) was also the father of Will Rogers, a famous humorist.

Left. A stone pipe with a beaver motif is similar to those used by the Cherokee. The stone was usually attached to softwood stems, which normally measured two feet long.

Right. A Cherokee pattern used on clothing.

Important Dates

1700: European settlers arrive in Cherokee Country.

1776: United States declares independence from Britain.

1821: Sequoyah presents his syllabary.

1828: Newspaper *Cherokee Phoenix* is published.

1830: Andrew Jackson signs Indian Removal Act.

1832: The Cherokee win Supreme Court decision over Georgia.

1835: Cherokee land ceded to U.S. against majority's wishes.

1838: Trail of Tears.

1861-65: U.S. Civil War.

1907: Oklahoma becomes the forty-sixth state.

1924: All Native Americans born in U.S. declared citizens.

1968: Indian Civil Rights Act gives Native Americans the right to govern themselves on their reservations.

1987: President Ronald Reagan establishes the Trail of Tears as a National Historical Trail.

PHOTO CREDITS

We want to extend a special thank you to Margie Douthit, Chester R. Cowen, Maggie Steber, Victoria Sheffler, Joan Greene, and Stephen Foster for all of their help in acquiring images for this book.

Pages 32-33: Tree and rocks, Photo by Dave Albers. Cherokee Chief, cropped, scene from "Unto These Hills," outdoor drama of the Cherokee, Cherokee, North Carolina, #D-65-79; operated by the Cherokee Historical Association.

Pages 34-35: Map by Susan Albers. Log cabin and boy, tinted vignette, scene from Oconaluftee Indian Village of Cherokee, North Carolina, Operated by the Cherokee Historical Association.

Pages 36-37: Newspaper, tinted, #20558.3, and Sequoyah, outlined, McKenney-Hall 1837 litho after 1828 painting by Charles Bird King, #20699.828, Courtesy of the Archives & Manuscripts Division of the Oklahoma Historical Society. Sequoia tree, Photo by Dave Albers.

Pages 38-39: Turtle rattle, Photo by Dave Albers, Courtesy of a Private Collection. Grandson and grandfather, cropped, Photo Courtesy of Maggie Steber, New York City, New York, #34. Teachers, cropped, Courtesy of the University Archives, John Vaughan Library, Northeastern State University, Tahlequah, Oklahoma, #0023.

Pages 40-41: Pot, Courtesy of Dover Books. Women potters, cropped and tinted, Courtesy of the Museum of the Cherokee Indian, Cherokee, North Carolina, #1034-A-4. Woman with circuit board, Courtesy of Maggie Steber, New York City, New York, #33.

Pages 42-43: Man making a canoe, Courtesy of the Oconaluftee Indian Village of Cherokee, North Carolina, #VP-12. Arrowhead, Photo by Dave Albers, Arrowheads handcrafted by Eddie Albers, Courtesy of a Private Collection. Man chipping arrowheads, tinted vignette, scene from Oconaluftee Indian Village of Cherokee, North Carolina, #V-25-59.

Pages 44-45: Committee, Courtesy of the University Archives, John Vaughan Library, Northeastern State University, Tahlequah, Oklahoma, # 209. Stone pipe, Photo by Dave Albers, Courtesy of a Private Collection. Pattern, Courtesy of Dover Books.

Pages 47-48: Graduates, Courtesy of the University Archives, John Vaughan Library, Northeastern State University, Tahlequah, Oklahoma. Mask, tinted and outlined, Courtesy of the Museum of the Cherokee Indian, Cherokee, North Carolina, #Ch. 188. Cherokee Alphabet, tinted, Courtesy of Sequoyah's Home Site, Sallisaw, Oklahoma, Administered by the Oklahoma Historical Society.

BIBLIOGRAPHY

Bleeker, Sonia. The Cherokee: Indians of the Mountains. New York: William Morrow & Co., 1952.

Brandon, Alvin M. The American Heritage Book of Indians. New York: American Heritage Publishing Co., 1961.

Brill, Marlene Targ. The Trail of Tears. Brookfield, CT: Millbrook Press, 1995.

Burt, Jesse and Robert B. Ferguson. Indians of the Southeast: Then and Now. Nashville: Abingdon Press, 1973.

Capps, Benjamin. The Old West: The Indians. New York: Time-Life Books, 1973.

Claro, Nicole. The Cherokee Indians. New York: Chelsea House Publishers, 1992.

Fleischmann, Glen. The Cherokee Removal, 1838. New York: Franklin Watts, 1971.

Fremon, David K. The Trail of Tears. New York: New Discovery Books, 1994.

Hirschfelder, Arlene and Martha Kreipe de Montano. Native American Almanac: A Portrait of Native America Today. New York: Prentice Hall, 1993.

Lepthien, Emilie U. The Cherokee. Chicago: Children's Press, 1985.

Lucas, Eileen. The Cherokees. Brookfield, CT: Millbrook Press, 1993.

Mancini, Richard E. Indians of the Southeast. New York: Facts on File, 1992.

Maxwell, James A., Editor. America's Fascinating Indian Heritage. Pleasantville, NY: Reader's Digest Association, 1978.

Perdue, Theda. The Cherokee. New York: Chelsea House Publishers, 1989.

Robbins, Mari Lu. Native Americans. Huntington Beach, CA: Teacher Crafted Materials, 1994.

White, Jon Manchip. Everyday Life of the North American Indian. New York: Holmes & Meier Publishers, 1979.

Woodward, Grace Steele. The Cherokees. Norman, OK: University of OklahomaPress, 1963.

Yannuzzi, Della A. Wilma Mankiller; Leader of the Cherokee Nation. Hillside, NJ: Enslow Publishers, 1994.

Above. 1901 graduates from the Cherokee Seminary, in Tahlequah, Oklahoma.

Right. A Cherokee dance mask carved in 1940 by Will West Long.

Bottom. The Cherokee were very skilled at using bow and arrows.

DSB
AGAYUH
Cherokee Alphabet (or Syllabary)

ᏧᎳᎦ ᏣᎳᎩ DSB
SEQUOYAH'S CHEROKEE ALPHABET

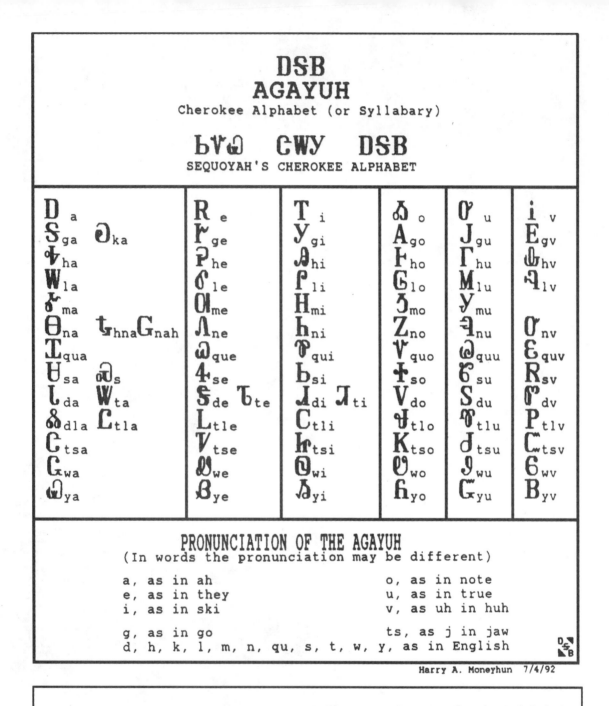

PRONUNCIATION OF THE AGAYUH
(In words the pronunciation may be different)

a, as in ah

e, as in they

i, as in ski

o, as in note

u, as in true

v, as uh in huh

g, as in go

ts, as j in jaw

d, h, k, l, m, n, qu, s, t, w, y, as in English

Harry A. Moneyhun 7/4/92

AGAYUH (a-ga-yuh)   Agayuh is an English word for the Cherokee alphabet invented by Sequoyah. The word is pronounced nearly the same in both Cherokee and English. 'Agayuh' is to Cherokee as 'alphabet' is to English. If a list of words were to be arranged in the sequence of the alphabet, they would be arranged from a through b to z. If a list of words were to be arranged in the sequence of the agayuh, they would be arranged from a through ga (down the columns), to yuh (yv).